Finding Kite

This choose your own adventure story is a unique, illustrated resource and a compelling mystery, focused on developing the social skills of children on the autistic spectrum. Trapped in Tudor England in 1535, in a world very different from their own, the reader must take on the role of the main character and work out why horses are mysteriously dying. Confronted by challenging social situations and decisions that will either help or hinder the narrative, they need to solve the mystery in order to get home.

The story provides a springboard for children to test out different actions and to experience a range of possible consequences and pathways. Decisions the reader must make tackle challenges such as working together and overcoming conflict, processing information and managing emotions and anxiety.

This book:

- is an engaging interactive story to enable discussion and create moments for deeper thinking and self-reflection;
- can be used either in small groups or 1:1 intervention;
- links directly to worksheets from the accompanying teacher resource, providing a personalised development tool that can be flexible according to the child's needs.

Although created with girls in mind, positioning the reader as the main character allows all children to become fully immersed in the narrative. This is an invaluable resource to develop social skills and build confidence among children aged 8–12.

Rachel Holmes works as a special educational needs coordinator (SENCo) within a specialist campus for secondary students with autism and associated mental health difficulties. She has previously set up a specialist unit for secondary students with autism within a mainstream setting and has led on primary curriculum development within an all-age special educational needs (SEN) school. Rachel has significant experience of providing in-service training (INSET) in both specialist and mainstream settings on a range of topics such as social communication, access to learning and sensory difficulties.

Finding Kite: A Social Skills Adventure Story

Rachel Holmes

Illustrated by Iain Buchanan

Routledge
Taylor & Francis Group

LONDON AND NEW YORK

First published 2021
by Routledge
2 Park Square, Milton Park, Abingdon, Oxon OX14 4RN

and by Routledge
52 Vanderbilt Avenue, New York, NY 10017

Routledge is an imprint of the Taylor & Francis Group, an informa business

British Library Cataloguing-in-Publication Data
A catalogue record for this book is available from the British Library

Library of Congress Cataloging-in-Publication Data
Names: Holmes, Rachel (Special educational needs coordinator), author.
Title: Finding Kite : a social skills adventure story/Rachel Holmes.
Description: Abingdon, Oxon; New York, NY: Routledge, 2021. |
Series: Adventures in social skills
Identifiers: LCCN 2020043540 (print) | LCCN 2020043541 (ebook) |
ISBN 9780367510350 (paperback) | ISBN 9781003052173 (ebook)
Subjects: LCSH: Social skills–Study and teaching (Elementary)–Juvenile literature. |
Social skills in children–Juvenile literature. | Decision making–Study and
teaching (Elementary)–Juvenile literature. | Decision making in children–Juvenile literature.
Classification: LCC HQ783 .H65 2021 (print) | LCC HQ783 (ebook) | DDC 302.3/4083–dc23
LC record available at https://lccn.loc.gov/2020043540
LC ebook record available at https://lccn.loc.gov/2020043541

ISBN: 978-0-367-51035-0 (pbk)
ISBN: 978-1-003-05217-3 (ebk)

Typeset in Helvetica
by Newgen Publishing UK

You're not leaving. No way. Not ever. You've looked forward to this all week and no one is going to stop you riding Kite. You've always loved horses and this year you've finally got your way and been allowed riding lessons. Every week the same plan: same day, same time, same result – you love it. So why does it have to be now, right now, that the stables have a power cut? Typical. All lessons are off.

You're beyond angry. The ground feels unsteady under your feet and the noises around you are deafening. Spinning, distorted faces are staring at you, breathing away your oxygen. It feels like you're suffocating. You long for Kite's steady, rhythmic trotting, the rhythm that calms and steadies your own – a ticking clock in a world of never-ending chaos. You've had enough. Enough of faces changing shape around you, enough of the panic whirling though your body, enough of listening to words that make no sense.

You run to Kite and jump on. You've always found it easy to communicate with her – no words are needed, just the gentlest of nudges. You're off, riding at last. The sound of hooves making music on the gravel instantly softens your rage. You've escaped. Your brain doesn't process the shouts from your parents behind, the pointless attempts to stop you. Your body and mind focus solely on the rhythm, a new heartbeat getting steadier and calmer. Steadier and calmer. Steadier and calmer.

You shut your eyes. The sound of gravel disappears as hooves sink gently and quietly into a grassy floor, leaving the stables far behind.

Peace.

Finally, you look up, calm. A woodland track, a field ahead – you have no idea where you are. In a panic you yank hard on the reins.

To your horror Kite rears up in shock. The rhythm is broken, you're tumbling to the ground and Kite is tumbling down next to you.

Your head pounds as you slowly sit up, spitting to remove granules of dirt from your mouth. Yuk. You've been an idiot: you're not a good enough rider to go out on your own and now your anger has hurt not just you but probably Kite as well. You reach out to stroke your companion as a way of saying sorry, but her skin feels different. It's courser, less groomed, patchy and rough. This isn't Kite and this isn't the woods. What's going on?

A strange stink, like garlic, fills your nose, making you gag. You look up to see a ceiling of wooden beams, like wonky prison bars closing you in. You look around, you're trapped.

This makes no sense. Where are you? Some kind of shed? A stable? Next to you a dark pony moans softly. She sounds sick and clearly needs help.

You reach in your pocket for your phone – time to face the music and ask your parents to pick you up. Perhaps the annoying tracking app they had installed will have its uses after all – at least the phone will know where you are, even if you don't.

A closed envelope flashes on your screen – new message – probably from your parents. You click open, and stare in shock at the words in front of you:

'Welcome to Tudor England. It's 1535, King Henry is on the throne – welcome to a whole new world. Time to use your passion for horses to solve a mystery. Horses at this stable have been dying – work out why and Kite will take you home. This world might look different, but people are still people. Decipher how to work with them and you'll succeed.'

The deafening sound of your thumping heartbeat is suddenly interrupted. Outside there are voices, getting louder. A man and a girl. The shouting suggests they are angry but you're struggling to follow the conversation.

What's going on? Where's Kite? More importantly, where are you? What should you do? The smell of garlic is making you feel sick, but you feel just as sick at the thought of meeting the strange-sounding people.

Interactions with new people can often feel stressful to you and so you avoid them when you can. You have no idea what you'll say to these people – though given it's a conversation that's about to happen 500 years ago in the past, maybe that's not important.

You take a deep breath and decide to go outside.

Turn to page 36.

You decide to trust your instincts. You don't know this person and as a matter of fact you hardly know Kit. It's not safe to be jumping on carts with people you don't know – you insist on walking.

The cart rolls past you. Kit flings her hands in the air and stomps the ground.

You hate arguments, but a stranger is a stranger. It just doesn't feel safe. You sneak another look at Kit's face. It's turned bright red. She's angry.

You stare at the ground, surrounded by an awkward silence that strangely seems to be hurting your ears.

If Kit's a real friend, she'll eventually understand … won't she … ?

After a near eternity Kit's head finally lifts and her eyes stare into yours. 'Come on,' she grimaces, 'no point wasting anymore time.' Kicking up a cloud of dust with her feet, Kit stomps off ahead, then pauses and checks you're following. Good news, no argument. You run to catch her up and walk on in peaceful silence.

Coming up, you see what you guess to be a farmhouse. You nearly vomit as you pass by mountains of manure piled high in the field next to you. Gross. What hurts your senses next though is worse – the sight of rows of dead chickens lying lifeless next to a farm cart. In shock you slowly realise they're in a worse state than death – they're alive but suffering horribly, waiting to be slaughtered. You had always thought animals had a hard time in modern times – but this is awful. Their legs have been tied together to stop them from escaping, their silence suggesting a resignation to their fate. You can't stop looking at their eyes. They're terrified.

Challenge

How might you feel in this situation? Do you have any beliefs or views that are really important to you?

Turn to page 27.

You've always found it easy to remember details and quickly find your way back to where you last left the girl. What was her name again, Kit?

She's not standing in the spot you last saw her. You look around and see a slumped body sitting on the grass under a tree.

You have no idea what to say to her.

As you're standing, trying to think, she looks up. 'There you are,' she mutters, her mouth making a slight frown squiggle. 'Why did you run?' she asked, her hands in front of her as if they were carrying an imaginary tray.

You don't know what to say. Kit really upset you by laughing. Is it OK to tell someone they made you upset? What if it makes them angry? What it if makes you angry again?

If you pretend everything is fine, turn to page 41.

If you decide to explain you didn't like her laughing at you and felt upset, turn to page 12.

'Horse seller?' he cries again. 'He's nothing but a criminal or a magic man. I traded four healthy pigs last week in exchange for a beautiful chestnut stallion. Full of life at the market, it was, full of beans.' (You're about to question the beans bit, sounds like a crazy diet for a horse, but you don't get the chance.)

'Didn't make the journey home,' continues Ade, 'dead within eight miles. Me and my sister tried talking with the seller, but we got nowhere – the horse looked perfectly fine when I bought it, everyone could see that. He tricked me, put a spell on that horse or something. No way it could be that sick and for me not to know.

I'm heading back to market to sell these last pigs – they're all we have left. Our harvest is ruined. With no horse we have no way of transporting our crops to market. Half of it's still in the barn too sodden now to sell.'

He looks down and you take the chance to study his face. The creases have gone and so too has the smile shape. Gravity seems to have suddenly gained strength – his mouth, chin and eyes are all being pulled down towards the ground. In fact, even his shoulders are being pulled downwards.

What's going on? How can healthy horses be dying so suddenly? You need to get to that market – and quickly.

You ask Ade for directions.

Challenge

Look at the strategies on page 43 to help you remember information you are told.

Ask for the directions to be read aloud to you. You will need to remember them.

When you are ready, recall the instructions by telling someone or writing them down.

When you can successfully describe the route to market yourself, turn to page 31.

Kit carries on talking, on and on and on. Even when you try, you can't really make sense of everything she's saying – too much information too fast. You start singing a song in your head to block out the words.

Your arm being tugged jolts you abruptly from your thoughts. 'Wake up,' Kit blurts crossly, 'you've not listened to a word I've said. I could really do with your help. I've no idea why this keeps happening – father thinks I'm not looking after the stallions properly but I am. I really am. If this horse dies, there's no way we can buy another one. There's no money left. You've got to help me find out what's happening to them.'

Well that's one piece of luck; despite not managing to follow everything she's said, it's clear she's on the same mission as you – and now she's the one asking you for help.

You agree to help and get squeezed tightly in response. Time to work as a team.

Hmm … easier thought than done … even agreeing step one seems impossible: Kit tells you she wants you to see the horse again in the shed and is convinced you'll somehow work out what's wrong. You think this is a stupid idea – you know nothing about what makes horses sick, the stables stinks and you've just escaped that angry man. You've no intention of meeting him again.

Surely it makes much more sense to go and find the person who sold them the horses? Maybe he or she can talk to Kit and see what's going so wrong. Wrong food? Dirty water? Too cold?

So how can you persuade her of your plan without upsetting her?

Challenge

Disagreeing with someone respectfully is tricky. Look at the phrases and body actions examples on page 42. Which are most likely to work best in this situation? Possible answers are at the bottom of the page.

If you picked the ones that often work well, turn to page 32.
If you picked different ones, turn to page 25.

The woman has already started to head down a small, dirty passageway away from the market. It's now or never. 'What do you mean?' you frantically shout after her, not caring in the slightest anymore what she thinks of you. 'Move away from the market, get out of sight,' she hollers back, before disappearing around a corner out of sight.

You start pushing your way back out of the crowd that has started to gather behind you. Thud! In horror you realise you've crashed into stocks. No way you're staying here a moment longer. Trying hard not to tread on the piles of rotting vegetables scattered around your feet, you head out round the edge of the market, flicking your fingernails to try and block out the sounds and smells. 'Duck Alley', perfect: a quiet, back street for you to escape down. You're desperate to slump down in a heap and rest, but you can hear people – you need to be well out of sight. You keep walking.

Up ahead you spy an area of deserted wasteland, away from the main market. A chance for peace at last. To your surprise you find three horses – sitting motionless, moaning gently and panting. They're clearly ill. You can see beads of sweat creeping down their manes and a river of slime coming from their noses. They need help. The quiet is broken by gentle sobs – cries from a girl, kneeling behind one of the horses, covering her face with her hands. The girl looks up. Kit!

Turn to page 20.

Kit listens as you explain how you feel, her face bending and scrunching as you talk, her eyes widening. 'So, you really are from the future? Amazing!' she shouts, her hands on her head. 'Incredible! A real-life adventure! So sorry for upsetting you, I just thought you were joking.'

Before you can reply, Kit takes your wrist and slides a daisy chain over your fingers. 'I've made you this. Friends?'

You feel much better. 'Friends,' you reply, smiling. You've been listened to.

Time to get to work.

'So, what's wrong with the horse in the stable?' you ask, hoping she'll give you clues of what's happening and suggest what you should to do next.

However, instead of a reply in words you get tears. Tears and more tears with no explanation.

Hmm. You have no idea what to do next. Ask more questions? Change the topic to something happier? Say nothing?

You walk on in silence.

'I can't bear to think of that horse dying as well,' Kit finally mumbles. 'Father bought two stallion horses in July, ready for breeding. Both died within weeks. He only bought this one yesterday and already he's sick.'

'Is that why you were arguing with the man?' you ask. (You're convinced he's the culprit behind all this.) Kit nods, a new tear gliding down her face, wiping away grime as it travels.

'He's my father,' says Kit, trying to choke back more tears. 'I wanted him to pay the blacksmith to come out, but we haven't got the money.'

You've stopped listening – distracted by the pattern of tiny dark spots on the soil being created by the tears.

Turn to page 9.

It turns out that Ade is heading to market too. Result, now he can you tell you the way.

You explain that you're looking for the horse seller, on a mission to find out why the horses are getting so sick. You still think it's something to do with Kit's father – maybe the seller can come back with you and find the clues you need.

His face suddenly changes. The big crescent smile is eaten up as his mouth widens. His forehead creases up. 'That crook!' he shouts. 'Horse seller? Horse killer more like.'

He's clearly upset. You start to feel anxious, not sure what's going on. You scrunch your toes to distract yourself and hum in your head to keep calm.

Turn to page 7.

Your mind is made up, you can't think about anything else. The world around you stops; no sounds, smells or sensations. You gently pull the first chicken towards you and with shaking hands untie the string. Something or someone is pulling you back, but no one stands a chance at stopping you. You're unaware as the chicken owner orders you to stop while charging towards you from the farmhouse ahead, unaware of the look of utter terror on Kit's face, or the splinters in your hand from the coarse string.

Chicken after chicken is released, your hands unlocking their freedom. Only when you reach the end do you suddenly process the chaos around you – a squawking, screeching mayhem, wings hitting every part of your body and claws scratching at bare skin. You must escape.

Turn to page 38.

You decide to keep your feelings to yourself and agree to the lift. You make your mouth and eyes go up to pretend you're excited, hoping Kit won't notice how red and hot you feel. The sound of hooves gets louder and louder, matching your pounding heartbeat. Two massive wooden wheels loom alongside you, it's now or never.

'Ok if we have a lift?' shouts Kit. 'Jump on,' grunts the man, not looking at all like the kindly family friend you'd tried picturing in your head. You scramble up, grab the wooden floor of the cart, your feet searching for a solid footing. You find a foot ledge and hang on, Kit giggling next to you. 'Thanks,' you shout across to the man when you've acclimatised to this new, strange form of transport, 'I'm a friend of Kit's, we're on a mission.' You're not even offered a grunt back. Rude.

You stop bothering with the man and focus on trying to listen to Kit, but she seems to be talking nonsense really. You're tired of acting excited and before long your mind drifts off to more interesting thoughts.

Deep in thought you don't hear the persistent alarm noise coming from the phone. Deep in thought you don't notice the look of panic creeping across Kit's face as you enter a barn. Deep in thought you don't notice the sound of wooden barn gates being locked behind you – until it's too late.

This isn't the market. You've been driven into a huge barn, pigeons squawking and flying high up to the rafters to escape the cartwheels. 'Kit, where are we?' you whisper. 'Is this your friend's farm?'

'I lied,' mumbles Kit quietly, 'I've no idea who he is or where we are. I was just so bored of walking.' Her head flops forward, her shoulders slump. You know you're in trouble.

Your phone beeps:

'Mission over.'

- Why do you think Kit lied about knowing this person?
- How might Kit have felt if you had said 'No'?
- Should we always agree with our friends?
- What should we do if we don't want to do something a friend suggests?
- Why can it be dangerous to trust people we don't know well?

Ready to try again? Turn to page 33. Good luck!

You have no idea what's happening, but you decide to give your brain a chance to think before you do anything else. You don't like the way the man shouted at you but walking away seems sensible until you know what's going on and who can help you.

You start to walk down a dusty track, desperate to escape the shouting. 'Wait,' cries the rotten-teeth girl, 'you're going the wrong way, the apples are down here. Come with me, I'll show you – my name's Kit by the way.'

'Apples?' you mutter, 'What's all the fuss about apples?'

The girl stops. 'You've come to pick the apples, haven't you? No? Well who are you then? And why are you wearing such strange clothes?'

Deep breath. You go for it and try to explain what's going on. 'You were just in the woods riding Kite … and then suddenly, well … here.' Blah blah blah. One minute in the real world … the next minute it's vanished. Tudor times????? You still can't take it in.

You look down, trying to block out this alien new world. Your eyes start to leak tears that sting.

Unbelievably, the girl laughs.

'Well that's certainly a good story,' she chuckles. She thinks you're lying. The laughing continues – chortling, snorting and half-finished sentences being interrupted by giggles.

Rage starts to build and burn in your body. You clench your hands tightly and punch them into your pockets. You're fuming with this girl. She's still laughing at you (with no care for how you feel) and hasn't believed a word you've said. How can she find it funny that you are this unhappy? You're about to tell her exactly what you think of her, when …

Beep beep! Your phone! The mission!

> 'Mission reminder … time is ticking. You're here to
>   solve a mystery remember. You'll need help.'

You normally prefer to work on your own; less stressful, less demanding, and less likely to lead to upset. You've tried working with people in the past and it's hard work, they constantly malfunction. You're fuming with this girl, but you have no idea how Tudor England works. What should you do?

If you decide to work alone, turn to page 22.

If you decide to try explaining how you feel before making a decision, turn to page 12.

You stand still, your thoughts tumbling across your brain. You clench your fists, desperately trying to stop your fingers from untying the string.

What to do?

'Oi, have you turned into a stone?' shouts Kit. You look up, amazed that she doesn't seem at all bothered about the suffering in front of her. In spurts and splutters you do your best to communicate your feelings of outrage, all the time trying to quell the beast of anger stomping inside your body. 'They're just chickens,' she replies, with a shrug and a yawn. You don't get it, why isn't she feeling the same as you? It's weird that she's so upset about horses being sick, but doesn't give a moment's thought to other animals.

You try to explain how you feel but it's hard – you're losing control of your voice; your heart is racing and your arms seem to be jerking around like a puppet on a string. Stop. Deep breaths. Deep breaths. OK, well breaths at least – it's a start.

You finally manage to explain that you desperately want to set them free. You don't get the response you wanted. A few phrases stick in your head: 'against the law', 'not making it to market to complete the mission', 'horses still suffering'.

That last one really registered. Reluctantly and sadly you decide to leave the chickens be. You're already on a mission and you've not got time to start this new one. The chickens will have to 'wait for another day' … only of course they can't.

Tears start to well in your eyes. You wish you could make others see the world the way you do.

You need time on your own. You run.

It's a shame you don't look back – you would have seen Kit wanting to help you feel better.

Turn to page 38.

You turn, ready to run away again – you're certain Kit must be angry with you for leaving earlier. Sure enough, she launches herself at you, but to your surprise she throws her hands around you and beams. 'Thank goodness you're OK, I've been looking everywhere,' she cries. 'These horses,' she shouts determinedly, 'they're sick, what can we do?' You try and order your thoughts, find some sort of plan but your brain freezes at the sight of the horse seller marching across the field. Kit pulls you back into the lane and you both crouch behind a pile of dung.

The overpowering smell of poo makes you start dreaming of a nose plug with different scents. Strangely your imagination becomes a reality in front of you as you stare in confusion at the horse seller: shouting aggressively and prodding the poor horses with a stick, he then pushes something into their noses. They jump up and sneeze an enormous sneeze – a slime river pouring out of their noses.

To your amazement, within seconds the horses no longer look sick; no more gunk and their legs are dancing, full of life. You crawl nearer, desperate to see the magic cure but an overwhelming smell stops you in your tracks. Garlic! He's shoved garlic up their noses so hard it has made them sneeze. They're not cured at all, it's just a trick to get rid of the slime for a few moments until he can sell them. Plus, they're not dancing – they're in pain, trying to escape their own noses. You watch in anger as the horse seller starts pushing them back down the lane towards the market, needing to sell them quickly while they look lively.

Cheat! Swindler! Criminal! He's selling sick horses. He's making a fortune out of misery and suffering.

You turn to Kit to tell her what you've seen but she's distracted by the noise of the market. You want to shout to get her attention but can't if you want to keep hiding unnoticed. You need her to listen … urgently.

Turn to page 39.

Better to go alone. This girl has laughed and laughed at you, and that's just about the worst feeling in the world. No point trying to work with someone who thinks it's funny to see you miserable.

You see a small, dirty path up ahead and make a run for it. Dirt and dust fly up around you like waves in the air. You close your eyes and keep running, coughing to keep the dirt away.

You have no idea where you're heading but feel calmer now you're on your own. You open your eyes and breathe. Every few seconds something new catches your eye and helps to distract you: a twig in the shape of a nose, a snail trail in the mud, a stinky puddle that's been taken over by hundreds of tiny flies, a leaf with a tear in the middle and two stone eyes peeping out from the grass.

Focus on the details, keep calm.

Focus on the details, keep calm.

It's working. You're calm …

Well you were, until you realise you have absolutely no idea where you are or what to do next.

Suddenly, without warning, pain shoots through your body and you crash face first into a mound of filth. Your foot is grabbed by the jaws of a faceless metal monster: an animal trap. Ouch.

You're lucky, it's only small and one side has already broken off. With a bit of wrestling you're free. You pat the ground around you, trying to find your phone that must have fallen out when you fell. Your eyes spot it before your hands – a bright screen flashes through the mud:

'Time to find some help. You can't solve this mystery on your own.'

Hmmm. Can you really sort things out with that girl? Only one way to find out. First hurdle – find the way back.

Can you remember the details you got distracted by? They will help you trace your steps. Once you've remembered them all, turn to page 6.

It's one thing deciding to make amends but quite another actually doing it. You hate speaking to people you don't know. What if your brain doesn't find any words to use? What if the words it does find make no sense? What if the words his brain picks make no sense either?

You start walking slowly towards him, hoping for a sink hole to suddenly appear and swallow him up. No such luck. You try and work out how near to get to him before starting the conversation – but your legs make the decision for you, they've turned into glue sticks and seem to have stuck to the ground. You keep your eyes rigidly fixed on the pigs' funny feet, to avoid looking at his face.

'Sorry,' you blurt out, 'I didn't mean to upset you, the pigs just made me laugh.' 'No, I'm sorry,' chuckles the boy, 'I'm just having a grumpy day, shouldn't have shouted at you. Those darned pigs are making me mad. I'm Ade, good to meet you.'

Well that interaction went well – and you feel proud to have sorted out the misunderstanding. Problem solved (well one at least).

Turn to page 13.

Your conversation doesn't go well.

Sometimes you find it's easier to copy others and agree with everything they say. That way no one spots if you're confused about what to do and you won't upset anyone. But this time, no way – there's no way you can go back to the stinking stable. You shout at Kit over and over – telling her the idea is stupid, the panic cooking inside you. Your mind is in fight or flight mode – you're prepared to fight this idea if you can, but if that doesn't work or you can't find the words, you'll run.

Your shouting is pointless. She has that strange, shocked face again and she seems to be ignoring everything you're saying. In fact, she's ignoring you completely – she's staring wide-eyed at something behind you.

You look round. It's the angry noise-machine man from the stable charging towards you. He must have heard the racket you've been making.

'I thought I told you to pick apples?' he roared, his face getting redder with every word. 'Think it's OK to ignore your elders, do you? My patience has run out. The cesspit needs emptying and while you're doing that you can spend some time thinking about respect.'

With the word 'cesspit' ringing in your ears you're marched back down the path. You don't notice the noise from your pocket of a new text message – perhaps it's a good job:

```
'No chance to solve horse mysteries while you're covered
              from head to toe in poo.'
```

'Mission over.'

> - In this scene you shouted your ideas to Kit to try and be listened to. How might this make Kit feel?
> - Think about times when someone disagreed with an idea you have had. How did they communicate this with you? How did you feel?
> - When people have different ideas it doesn't mean that one idea is definitely right and one is definitely wrong. Can you think of some examples?

Ready to try again? Turn to page 42. Good luck!

Anger rages through your body, finding nowhere to escape or be processed. You have always been passionate about animal rights. You feel sick.

Kit seems oblivious and has started moaning again about the long walk. All you can see are chicken eyes. Rows upon rows of beady eyes staring up at you. Are they pleading for help? You're their only hope.

What should you do?

If you decide to act fast and release the chickens immediately, turn to page 14.

If you decide to wait a few minutes and think through what to do, turn to page 19.

3, 4

You decide to confront the crazy, shouty man. (Though, to be honest, you didn't really 'decide' anything. Your body has a habit of launching into action faster than you can think: brain and body never quite in sync.) His shouting is piercing your ears so hard they hurt. You need it to stop. You march up to the man, ready to fight back.

'You crazy idiot,' you scream (ironically louder than his shouting, not that you notice). You expect the man to listen or apologise even, but to your surprise and shock he shows no sign of hearing anything you say. Instead he shakes his head, walks over to a gate, holds it open and tells you (rudely) to leave.

Still shouting, you march out of the gate and carry on going, occasionally shouting back at the man to make sure he knows what you think of him. Eventually, when calm, you stop. You have no idea where you are and there is no one in sight to help. You reach for your phone but to your horror you realise it's gone – must have fallen out while you were busy shouting.

Temper lost. Phone lost. Mission lost ...

'Mission over.'

- Who did the man think you were? Why was he cross?
- Being shouted at like this isn't OK. It is likely to make us feel upset or worried. What could we do to stay calm ourselves?
- Challenging people who act in an unkind way is important. However, why do we sometimes need to walk away from situations even when the other person is in the wrong?
- Who could you talk to if someone is unkind to you?

Ready to try again? Turn to page 37. Good luck!

You're terrified. The fight is getting worse – more and more people are joining in and an even bigger crowd is gathering to watch. 'Lie low' was what she said, but it makes no sense. You realise you should have asked her to explain. She was clearly trying to help. You look round, but she's gone. Only one thing you can do now – you'll just have to 'lie low'.

You push through the crowds, hands finally finding a wall rather than people. You edge along the buildings, struggling to think. You slump against the wall of a house and do what you were told – lie down as low as possible. What now? Your mind wanders to the start of this madness. How did you end up in this mess?

You stare up at the sky above you (trying to distract yourself away from the noise and chaos around you). It seems so normal – sky, birds, clouds. Your phone must hold the solution to your escape. Your phone told you your mission, what other information is on it?

Just as you get your phone out of your pocket, a woman screams at you from a window above. 'Move on, urchin. This isn't a hotel you know, you're not sleeping on my doorstep,' and with that, a pail full of sewage falls from the sky. Disgusting. Gross. You feel sick. Of all the houses to lie next to, you pick the one with the fullest toilet pail inside. Not such a normal sky after all then.

You reach for your phone. It's soaked. Battery dead.

'Mission over.'

- Do you ever find people use strange phrases to communicate? What do you do when you don't understand what someone has said?
- Why is it sometimes hard to ask for help?

Ready to try again? Turn to page 31. Good luck!

You thank Ade for his help and walk on, trying to remember each step of the directions, enjoying the silence and peace. You desperately want to zone out, by replaying your favourite advert in your head or singing a song, but you manage to stay focused – chuckling at the irony of the phrase 'lost in thought', a literal reality you definitely need to avoid.

Yuk. Suddenly, the stench of poo is everywhere. You look up. You've arrived … but this is like no market you've ever seen.

A huge, muddy square looms ahead. Buildings of every shape and size surround the edges, squeezed into even the tightest of spaces. Wonky wooden beams seem to push against the walls, jostling for breathing space. Cattle, sheep, pigs, ducks, chickens all bellow and protest in outrage at being rammed into tiny, claustrophobic pens. So many people. You feel sick and struggle to fight the urge to escape, run back to the empty fields and hide. Pushing, shoving, spitting, arguing, cackling, running, staring, glowering … too many movements to make sense of. The ground is spinning. You need a trap door.

Up ahead a fight breaks out. You are terrified. The sun's reflection from a sword bounces painfully into your eyes and the sound of metal pierces through the chaos.

'Looks like trouble,' mutters a young woman next to you. You have no idea if she's talking to you or just herself and look up at her face to search for clues. 'Best lie low eh,' she offers next, nodding her head in your direction.

You have no idea what this means and don't want to ask her to explain in case she thinks you're stupid or starts a complicated conversation.

What do you do?

If you decide to risk embarrassment and ask her what she means, turn to page 10.

If you decide to work it out yourself, turn to page 29.

Great, you've explained your point well, and on this occasion, you've convinced her to change her mind.

Kit explains that her father bought all three horses from a seller in Smithfield – the biggest market for miles. It is also miles away … and the only transport is the pair of legs attached to your body. Tudor life sucks. 'Well don't just stare at your feet: use them,' urges Kit, 'we need to move. The sun's already high in the sky – the market won't be on much longer today. If we miss it, we'll have to wait until next week.' Next week? Your feet suddenly have no problem moving.

You march on, trying not to stumble on the bumpy ground, searching for signs of a market ahead. Nothing.

You hear horse hooves behind you and turn to see a red-faced man driving a horse and cart. 'We're in luck,' shouts Kit excitedly, 'I know him. He'll be off to sell his chickens. Let's see if he'll give us a ride. You'll love it, it's fun being on this adventure with you.'

You don't know what to do. Although you'd love a ride to market instead of all this walking, this person's a stranger. You don't know him, and you certainly don't know if it's safe. You look at Kit, wanting to tell her you'd rather walk, but you can see she's excited and wants the ride. You're worried about telling her how you feel. What will she think of you?

You don't know what to do. It's difficult to fit in with other people, you don't want to lose this new friend already. Should you hide your feelings – and copy the excited look on Kit's face?

If you decide to accept a ride, turn to page 15.

If you decide to tell Kit you want to carry on walking, turn to page 4.

The boy seems cross with you and you have no real idea what to say next. Whatever you say, you know he will say something back, and then you'll have to think of something else, and then more and more, and it just gets too confusing and muddled. Blah blah blah – brain freeze. If you knew in advance what he was going to be thinking at each point and what he was about to say, then you could manage much better – but right now you can do without the stress.

In any case, you're here to solve a mystery, not waste time making friends. Right?

You start singing out loud to block out any further words he might throw at your ears and stride off as fast as you can in the direction of the market. It's just a shame you don't know which direction that should be …

After 20 minutes of walking aimlessly across three fields, with no sign of life on the horizon, reality hits: you need help. No internet maps to help you here – and yes, you did check on the phone.

No alternative – you will have to go back and try to get the boy to help.

Challenge

What could you say to the boy? Try and think of an opening sentence.

When you are ready, turn to page 24.

You can't stay in the strange shed a minute longer. The smell of garlic is climbing up your nose and down your throat. If you wait any longer you will be sick. Feeling scared you creep outside. You suck in the delicious oxygen air outside and for a tiny moment your mind is still.

Without warning, a man shouts in your ear, causing you to flinch in pain: 'Hey you, you're late. You were meant to start work in the orchard at dawn. Lazy, good for nothing urchin.' All you can do is stare – stare at his filthy, ragged clothes, stare around you at the strange, thatched huts, stare at the horse and cart in the distance ahead. The world hasn't just changed – most of it has disappeared.

'Oi, you listening?' the voice carries on. 'The apples won't pick themselves. Move it.'

You have no idea what he is talking about.

Behind the noise-maker man a girl is staring at you, her mouth wide open, releasing a waft of foul-smelling breath. Her eyes are also wide open, her eyebrows raised high like they're trying to escape her face. Why is she making such a strange face?

At least one thing is clear – you dislike this man immensely. Not only is he bossing you around with no right, but you assume he must also be responsible for the terrible state of the poor horse. He needs to stop.

So, what should you do?

If you decide to shout back at the man and tell him exactly what you think of him, turn to page 28.

If you decide to keep your thoughts inside for a while and walk away, turn to page 17.

You run as fast as you can, making your heart beat louder than the thoughts in your head. You wish you could run home – but for now just running feels good.

Only problem is that you've now run away from the one person who was trying to help you. Surely the mission is doomed.

Up ahead you spot a boy trying to persuade a crowd of pigs to move, unsuccessfully. You find yourself studying the creatures, with their funny, quirky features. It's a comedy sight. You've seen sheep herding, but pig herding? Seriously?! Despite everything that's just happened, you chuckle – in fact, not just chuckle, but properly snort and laugh. Pig versus man (well boy): who'd have thought the pigs would be winning.

'Oi,' shouts the boy crossly, 'think it's OK to laugh at people, do you?' He's got it wrong. You weren't trying to make fun of him. It just looks such a funny sight. You're reminded of how you reacted to Kit's laughter when she first met you. The phrase 'crossed wires' starts to make sense – shame he can't see inside your brain to see what you're thinking.

What should you do?

If you decide to try and make amends with the boy, turn to page 24.
If you decide to walk away, turn to page 34.

'Quick,' you hiss urgently to Kit, your face stretching as wide as you can to get her attention, 'get help.' Kit looks baffled – having missed the details you've witnessed. You watch her face twist and dance as you tell her what you've seen. She runs from sight, darting back into the market crowd, before returning with a confused looking sergeant. She's frantically explaining what's happened, her face stretching up and down in time with her words. You watch as the sergeant's expression changes – from confusion to sternness, from disinterest to determination. Good, he's listening.

Moments later you watch with delight, as the horse seller is marched to the centre of the square, crowds parting like a zip in front of him.

Looks like the stocks will be getting used today after all … shame the rotten tomato throwing can't be exchanged for garlic … you know where you would put it …

Your daydreaming is interrupted by the familiar beep of your phone:

`'Mystery solved. Mission accomplished! You've done it!'`

Pride surges through your body. You think of all the skills you've gained on your journey and the problems you have solved. You've been able to manage your own emotions brilliantly, think about the emotions of others and communicate your feelings to work in a team. The sound of hooves jolts you from your thoughts and you look up.

It's Kite.

You gasp and turn around to tell Kit what's happened, but behind you is only woodland. You look ahead – more woodland …

You're going home … !

(Psst … Want one last challenge? Turn to page 44.)

You're still upset that Kit laughed at you and thinks you're lying – but you can't find the words to tell her. What if she starts laughing at you again? Or gets cross? Maybe you did something wrong that you don't know?

You tell Kit you're sorry for running off. Kit shrugs and give you a hug. It should make you feel happy, but it doesn't. You feel lonely and sad that you haven't communicated how you feel. Kit has no idea – if anything, she still seems a bit cross with you.

You often pretend everything is fine and don't make a fuss when friends upset you. You wonder whether this is a good idea or not? You certainly don't feel happy right now.

You decide to try again.

When you can finish the following sentence to communicate how you feel, turn to page 12: 'Thanks for the hug. Actually, I wanted to tell you …'

Challenge: 'nope … nah … no way'

Which of these phrases might help you disagree respectfully?

A   'Your idea is ridiculous. There's no point telling me about it.'
B   'I'm not sure about your idea. Tell me your plan again.'
C   'I can see why you like that idea. Let me explain mine and see what you think.'
D   'I hate that idea, I thought you were my friend. Clearly not.'
E   'No way am I doing that. Either listen to my idea or go on your own.'
F   'Are you mad? That's stupid.'
G   'If you won't do it my way then we can never be friends.'
H   'Your idea could definitely work for some people, but I'm not sure it's a good plan for me because …'

What body language and actions often work best?

1.   Arms crossed.
2.   Looking towards the person.
3.   Frowning.
4.   Waving arms around.
5.   Speaking calmly.
6.   Tutting.
7.   Pointing.
8.   Nodding.
9.   Laughing.
10. Standing still.
11. Shouting.
12. Listening.

Now turn back to page 9.

Answers: B, C, H, 2, 5, 8, 10, 12

Challenge: 'memory lane'

Ask someone to read out the directions at the bottom of this page. It can be tricky to remember lots of information. You could try some of these techniques:

- Imagine you are walking the route as it is described: what might you smell, hear and see?
- Imagine an animal doing something funny at each place (e.g. a lion, elephant, crocodile, hedgehog).
- Draw the route so you can use it as a map or act it out.
- Ask for it to be repeated in sections so you can practise the route in your head.
- Pack an imaginary packed lunch and drop a piece of food at each place described.
- Imagine the weather changing at each place described (e.g. a rainbow, snow, sunshine).
- Read the directions and highlight important information.

Directions:

1. Follow the path down there until you get to the hogbog*. Watch out for the pig muck.
2. Turn left and carry on until you get to the oak tree with the branch leaning over the path.
3. Take a short cut by turning right until you get to the stream.
4. Jump across the shallow section and walk through the wheat fields.
5. When you get to the barn turn left and carry on down the path until you see the stone tower.
6. Turn right and walk through the tiny stone arch. You'll see the market in front of you.

* A house for pigs and chickens

When you can successfully remember the directions, turn to page 31.

43

Making a good impression – Tudor style!

Humans throughout history have always found ways to connect to others and build relationships. Listening, communicating and having respect for others are important skills, whatever year we are in. However, the way we socialise with people changes over time.

Would you make a good first impression in Tudor times? Let's find out.

True or false?

1. If you are invited to dinner you must take your own cutlery.
2. If you need to blow your nose, make sure you use a handkerchief.
3. Football would be a good game to play with your new friends.
4. Make sure you have some moss; it could come in handy.
5. Make sure you remember to flush the toilet after you've used it.
6. If you want to be on time, listen for the bells.
7. Wear purple if you want to impress.
8. Be prepared to share your plate of food with others.
9. You won't find toothpaste so don't be surprised if you get black teeth.
10. Make sure you have a regular bath.

Answers

1. True … but don't take a fork, they weren't used until the late sixteenth century.

2. False … it was rare to have a handkerchief so blow your nose straight towards the floor and tread any mess into the ground … yuk!

3. False … King Henry tried to ban it. In any case, it was often very violent and the goals could be in different villages! Plus, you would need to make a football first – often from a pig's bladder.

4. True … it was used instead of toilet paper! If you can't find moss you could try hay, sheep wool or leaves.

5. False … most people would have used a hole in the ground or a bowl. However, the first modern-day version of a flushing toilet was invented in Tudor times – by the godson of Elizabeth I. It was apparently very noisy!

6. True … clock towers in towns would ring bells to help people know the time. Some towers had clock faces as well – but only an hour hand, so good luck working out an accurate time. If you can't find a clock you could always use the sun.

7. Hmm … well that depends – are you related to royalty? Only the king and his family could wear purple in Tudor times. Perhaps stick to undyed beige cloth if you don't want to attract a lot of questions!

8. True … if you get invited to a banquet you will probably share your plate with three or four other people and your cup with the person next to you. Be prepared to try a few new dishes – you might have swan or seal on the menu.

9. False … people knew that keeping teeth clean was important. Sugar was far too expensive for most people, so it was mainly the super-rich who had black teeth. (Though actually you could have black teeth every morning if you want to – many people cleaned their teeth with soot.)

10. False … baths were thought to be dangerous in case they let bad air into the skin. Staying clean was important though – so make sure you wash your linen and clothes as often as possible. If that fails, try wafting some sweet-smelling herbs around your home to reduce the smell!